William C. Devecmon

In Re Shakespeare's Legal Acquirements

William C. Devecmon

In Re Shakespeare's Legal Acquirements

ISBN/EAN: 9783337058203

Printed in Europe, USA, Canada, Australia, Japan

Cover: Foto ©Thomas Meinert / pixelio.de

More available books at **www.hansebooks.com**

CONTENTS.

iii

IN RE SHAKESPEARE'S LEGAL ACQUIREMENTS.

I.

SHAKESPEARE NOT NECESSARILY A LAWYER BECAUSE HE USED LEGAL TERMINOLOGY.

ENGLAND is, and always has been, the true home of the lawyer; and the Englishman takes as naturally to a legal contest as the Irishman to a rough and tumble fight, or the Frenchman to a duel. In no country in the world have the bench and the bar been held in so high esteem as in England. While in all other parts of Europe the pulpit or the sword afforded the only avenues of employment for a gentleman, and the only means for social or political advancement, in England ambition has always found an ample arena in the legal forum. Prior to the reign of Queen Anne, science, literature, and art were lightly regarded, but the lawyer has always been, in English estimation, second only to the soldier. Bacon himself was esteemed by his contemporaries for his legal rather than his scientific or literary attainments. Hooker's famous statement that "law hath her seat in the bosom of God; her voice is the harmony of the world," has ever been applied literally by Englishmen to the Common Law. A love of law, a spirit of litigation, a tenacious and pertinacious determination to maintain his legal rights at all hazards and at every cost are characteristics of every trueborn Englishman. Von Ihering, in his remarkable work, " The Struggle for Law," to which I shall have occasion hereafter to refer, says " We [on the Continent] frequently see the typical figure of the traveling Englishman who resists being duped by innkeepers and hackmen, with a manfulness which would induce one to think he was defending the law of Old England—who, in case of need, postpones his departure, remains days in the place, and spends ten times the amount he refuses to pay. The people laugh at him, and do not understand him. It were better if they did understand him. For, in the few shillings which the man here defends, Old England lives."

The English love for law, and even for its intricacies, subtleties, and fictions is visible in all English history and literature. Blackstone's " Commentaries" were written, not for professed students of law, but as an advanced course of study for the English gentleman. The fascination that courts and the law had for Dickens is manifest throughout his novels, while Dr. Johnson never ceased to regret that he had not actively embraced the legal profession; but these are mere illustrations, and to multiply instances of this kind were tedious. This English characteristic is manifest in every age of English life; it is pre-eminently so in the Elizabethan era. Then was witnessed the great struggle between the Common Law and Chancery. The recently enacted Statute of Uses was the occasion of a great multitude of cases involving the title to real estate. It was emphatically an age of litigation. And the spirit of their race and times seized strongly on the Shakespeare family. There was a fortnightly court held at Stratford-on-Avon; and though all its records have not been preserved, it appears, from such as remain, that John Shakespeare, from his first settlement in that town about 1551 or 1552 down to 1600, was engaged either as plaintiff or defendant in nearly fifty law-suits. Besides he frequently served as juror, assessor of fines, and as arbitrator. His son, the future poet, was thus brought up in an atmosphere of litigation. That the little provincial town of Stratford, having at that time about 1800 inhabitants, with little or no commerce or intercourse with the outside world, was able to support a half dozen or more attorneys, with a session of court every two weeks, shows a most extraordinary amount of litigation. It may well be imagined that the greater part of the male population of Stratford was in constant attendance at the sessions of the court; that the arguments of the lawyers, the verdicts of the juries, and the judgments of the court were in the long evenings rehashed over and over again by these worthies of Stratford in the midst of their potations of home-brewed ale, in the love of which they excelled no less than in the love of litigation, there being at the time about thirty alehouses in the town.

John Shakespeare was a man of prominence and importance in Stratford, for twenty years holding office of one kind or another; and, as high bailiff, he presided over the court.

From these circumstances it can readily be seen how Shakespeare acquired his extensive knowledge of legal expressions, and his love of litigation which involved him in almost as many law-suits as his father. It is noticeable that, while Shakespeare's works abound with law-terms, they are devoid of terms peculiarly applicable to Chancery practice or to Chancery jurisprudence. The High Court of Chancery sat at London; the management of a suit therein was expensive; and Shakespeare had no opportunity of attending its sessions. His father had two suits in that court, but apparently they were abandoned, he being the complainant in both cases.

Such being the surroundings of Shakespeare's youth, in a bookless community, with a school where " small Latin and less Greek," and no English at all, were taught, it might well be imagined that a bright, intellectual boy would find the best educational facilities were to be had by a faithful attendance at the sessions of court. And when we consider that Shakespeare's father was almost constantly there, and when we further consider his own evident fondness for the law, shown not only in his use of legal expressions, but in his frequent resort to the courts as litigant, his legal tastes and fondness for legal terminology are accounted for. But that he got this terminology wrong quite as often as he got it right is apparent to any serious examination: certainly it is apparent to any lawyer not tempted by an appetite for *tours de force*, or burning to make a fellow-barrister out of the greatest of dramatists!

When he arrived in London and was thrown into that brilliant society of lawyer-playwrights, he continued to breathe the same legal atmosphere in their company at the taverns. Gifford, in his " Memoirs of Ben Jonson," says, " Domestic entertainments were, at that time, rare. The accommodations of a private house were ill calculated for the purposes of a social meeting, and taverns and ordinaries are therefore almost the only places in which we hear of such assemblies." The contemporary authority as to these meetings of the lawyers at the taverns is also ample. Dekker, in his " Gull's Hornbook " (1609) says: " There is another ordinary at which your London usurer, your stale bachelor, and your thrifty attorneys do resort; the price, three-pence; the rooms as full of company as a gaol. . . If they chance to discourse, it is of nothing but statutes, bonds, recognizances, audits, subsidies, rents, sureties, enclosures, liveries, indictments, outlawries, feoffments, judgments, commissions, bankrupts, amercements, and of such horrible matter."

That the poets and actors of the period were deep drinkers, and that " The Mermaid " and other taverns and tippling houses were their customary meeting places, are matters of common knowledge. Chapman's " temperance " was noted as a quality rarely met with in a poet.—Warton's " Hist. Eng. Poetry," vol. iv., p. 276.

To meet there and exchange jest and witticism in the midst of their "bumpers" was their ideal of pleasure and good-fellowship. In Dekker's "A Knight's Conjuring," 1607, a number of poets are introduced together in the Elysian fields. " Beyond all these places there is a groave which stands by itself like an iland—— This is called *The Groave of Bay-trees*, and to this consort-room resort none but the children of Phœbus, poets and musitians." To this Company is admitted Chettle, "sweating and blowing by reason of his fatnes, to welcome whom, because he was of old acquaintance, all rose up and fell presentlie on their knees to drink a health to all lovers of Helicon."

> What things have we seen
> Done at the Mermaid! heard words that have been
> So nimble, and so full of subtle flame,
> As if that every one from whence they came
> Had meant to put his whole wit in a jest,
> And had resolved to live a fool the rest
> Of his dull life.
> —Francis Beaumont to Ben Jonson.

> Souls of Poets dead and gone,
> What Elysium have ye known,
> Happy field or mossy cavern,
> Choicer than the Mermaid Tavern?
> —Keats.

But members of the legal profession were quite as frequent visitors to the taverns as the poets. For this we have a vast body of contemporary testimony. In Webster's "The Devil's Law Case," Sanitonella, a lawyer, complains,

There's one thing too that has a vile abuse in it.

Pros. What's that ?

San. Marry, this,—that no proctor in term-time be tolerated to go to the tavern above six times i' the forenoon.

—Act V. scene 2.

This same play also furnishes evidence that it was not merely the lawyers who were interested in legal gossip.

San. Do you hear, officers ?
You must take special care that you let in
No brachygraphy-men [*i. e.*, stenographers] to take notes.

Off. No, Sir ?

San. By no means :
We cannot have a cause of any fame
But you must have scurvy pamphlets and lewd ballads
Engendered of it presently.

—Act IV. scene 2.

Sidney Lee, in his life of " William Shakespeare," p. 32, n. 2, says, " Legal terminology abounded in all plays and poems of the period," the truth of which statement must be admitted by everyone at all familiar with Elizabethan literature. The whole population seems to have taken an interest in law and litigation. " Every man in those days was to a certain point his own lawyer; that is, he was well versed in all the technical forms and procedure. Therefore Counsel were brought into very close relations with their somewhat exacting clients, by whom they might be said to be chiefly instructed, the solicitor or attorney being rather in the position of an agent for the general conduct of cases "

(Hubert Hall's " Society in the Elizabethan Age," 2d Edition, p. 141).

That Shakespeare uses legal expressions rather more frequently than his contemporaries simply proves that he entered into the spirit of his times more fully than they. Wordsworth says of Milton that " his soul was like a star, and dwelt apart "; but Shakespeare was verily " the soul of his age," as Ben Jonson aptly described him, and, being its soul, he did not live apart from it, but in the very centre and the midst of it!

John Webster was a contemporary of Shakespeare. His father was a merchant tailor, and he himself is supposed to have followed that trade. In his play above mentioned, " The Devil's Law Case," occur more legal expressions (some of them highly technical, and all correctly used), than are to be found in any single one of Shakespeare's works. Among other legalisms, the law in regard to *pre-contract* (of which such capital is made by those who ascribe to Shakespeare great legal knowledge) is stated more fully than it is by Shakespeare, and quite as accurately. Webster doubtless acquired his knowledge of law in the same way in which I believe Shakespeare acquired his—that is, he absorbed it from the legal atmosphere by which he was surrounded.

But, if the law was attractive to the poets, the stage seems to have had an equal fascination for the lawyers. Indeed, the ranks of the dramatists were largely recruited from the Inns of Court.

There were contemporary with Shakespeare perhaps between seventy-five and a hundred writers of plays, and some of them were very prolific. Thomas Heywood said he "had either an entire hand or at least a main finger" in two hundred and twenty plays. Many were the authors of but one. A large percentage of the dramatic literature of the period has not survived to modern times, and of most of the authors also only their names remain. Of those who are known to have had any trade, professional training, or occupation, I believe it would be a conservative estimate a say that twenty per cent. were in some way connected with the study of law.

John Ford (1586-1640) came of a family of lawyers. His mother was a sister of Sir John Popham, next to Coke the most famous lawyer of his age. He became in turn Attorney-General and Lord Chief Justice. Ford himself was a student in the Middle Temple in 1602, while his cousin and namesake (to whom he dedicated " The Lover's Melancholy ") was a member of Gray's Inn.

John Marston (1575-1634) was a student of the law. His father, a lecturer at the Middle Temple in 1592, by his will, proved in 1599, bequeaths "to sd. son John my furniture &c. in my chambers in The Middle Temple; my law books &c. to my sd. son whom I had hoped would have profited by them in the study of the law, but man proposeth and God disposeth."—Introduction to Bullen's " Marston," p. 13.

Francis Beaumont (1584-1616) was a student in the Inner Temple. His grandfather, John Beaumont, had been Master of the Rolls; and his father, Francis Beaumont, one of the Judges of the Court of Common Pleas.

William Warner (1558?-1609) was "by his profession an atturnye at the Common Plese." He was the author of "Albion's England," and of a play called "Syrinx." In 1595 his translation of Plautus' "Menæchmi" was published. Shakespeare is said to have taken his "Comedy of Errors" from this play, and if he wrote it before 1595 (which seems probable) it is possible he may have seen Warner's translation in the manuscript. (See Dr. Morgan's Introduction to vol. xxii. of "The Bankside Shakespeare.")

Abraham Fraunce (15 -16) was a lawyer; had been a student at Gray's Inn; and was recommended by Henry, Earl of Pembroke, to Lord Treasurer Burleigh in 1590 as a suitable person to be Her Majesty's Solicitor in that Court. He was the author of several dramatic pieces.

Thomas Middleton (1570?-1627) was a student at Gray's Inn.

Thomas Lodge (1558-1625) was a student at Lincoln's Inn. Afterwards he became a physician.

Thomas Kyd (15 -1596) was trained for his paternal profession of a law scrivener.

The above facts, as well as those given below of plays represented at the Inns of Court, may be easily verified by reference to Ward's " History of English Dramatic Literature," and to the well-known " Biographia Dramatica."

Only those lawyer-dramatists have been mentioned whose ages were such as to render it probable that they came in contact with Shakespeare at some of the well-known taverns which were the common places of resort. Doubtless a fuller investigation than I have made would discover others.

Plays and masques were frequently represented at the different Inns of Court, sometimes in Latin, and nearly always written expressly for the occasion. The earliest English tragedy, " Ferrex and Porrex," said to be " the first dramatic piece of any consideration in the English Language," was acted on January 18, 1562, by gentlemen of 'the Inner Temple before the Queen. It was written by Thomas Sackville, afterwards Lord Buckhurst, and Thomas Norton, barristers. The latter subsequently became Counsel to the Stationers' Company.

In 1566 two plays by George Gascoigne of Gray's Inn, " Jocasta " and " Supposes," were there represented. In the composition of the former he was assisted by Christopher Yelverton, who afterwards arose to Judicial dignity.

" Tancred and Gismonda," under its original title of " Gismonda of Salerne," was represented before the Queen at the Inner Temple in 1568. It was written by Cristopher Hatton and five other gentlemen of the Inner Temple.

" The Misfortunes of Arthur " was acted before the Queen in 1588. Eight members of the Society of Gray's Inn co-operated in its composition; and four other gentlemen of the Inn, one of whom was

Francis Bacon, devised the dumb shows introducing the several acts.

Francis Bacon also contributed to " The Prince of Purpoole," which was represented at Gray's Inn in 1594.

In 1594 Shakespeare's " Comedy of Errors " was represented at Gray's Inn; and, in 1601, his " Twelfth Night " at the Inner Temple. (See Appleton Morgan's Introduction to vol. xxii. of " The Bankside Shakespeare.")

In 1612 a masque by George Chapman was produced by members of the Middle Temple and Lincoln's Inn; and one by Francis Beaumont by the members of the Inner Temple and Gray's Inn in 1613. (See Morley's Introduction to " Jonson's Masques," Carisbrooke Library, p. 23.)

The above, of course, is not a complete list of such representations. " In those days . . . the Inns of Court vied with each other in masques and pageants as much as in the record of Chancellors and Chief Justices " (Strachey's Introduction to " Beaumont and Fletcher," Mermaid Series, p. 13).

II.

HOW SHAKESPEARE HAS BEEN MADE A LAWYER.

It was the custom in Shakespeare's time for youth to leave school at fourteen or fifteen years of age; and it cannot be supposed that William attended school after reaching that age, in 1579. To account for what he did from then until 1586 has been a fruitful source of speculation for his biographers. There are traditions that he was apprenticed to a butcher, a glover, and nearly all the trades followed at Stratford, but none that he was an attorney or an attorney's clerk. But his enthusiastic biographers felt under the necessity of accounting for these years when no scrap has been found to throw any light upon his life except the memoranda relative to the publication of the banns for his marriage and the birth of his children, and as each new biographer felt that he must add some new suggestion in order to distinguish himself from his predecessors, it was finally, in 1790, by Malone, supposed that he might have been a clerk in an attorney's office, thus killing two birds with one stone, and accounting not only for the barren seven years, but for the legal expressions to be found in his works. This new idea was eagerly taken up, and in 1858, Mr. T. Payne Collier sought the opinion of Lord

Campbell, the eminent author of " The Lives of the
Chief Justices " and of " The Lives of the Lord
Chancellors," who replied, in part, as follows:
" Were an issue tried before me as Chief Justice at
the Warwick assizes whether William Shakespeare,
late of Stratford-upon-Avon, gentleman, ever was
a clerk in an attorney's office in Stratford-upon-
Avon aforesaid, I should hold that there is evidence
to go to the jury in support of the affirmative, but
I should add that the evidence is very far from
being conclusive, and I should tell the twelve gentlemen in the box that it is a case entirely for their
decision—without venturing even to hint to them,
for their guidance, any opinion of my own. Should
they unanimously agree in a verdict either in the
affirmative or negative, I do not think that the
court, sitting *in banco*, could properly set it aside
and grant a new trial."

The learned Lord Chancellor then proceeds to
give his views in detail, and though he says that
if the issue were tried before him he would not
venture even to hint to the jury an opinion of his
own, he has no such scruples when addressing Mr.
Collier or the readers of his published book; he
scorns the idea that the " gentle Shakespeare "
could have been engaged in killing calves or work-
ing in leather, and thinks it highly improbable that
he could have followed any meaner occupation than
that of an attorney's clerk, and adds " perhaps his
employer sent him up to the metropolis to conduct
suits before the Lord Chancellor or the superior
courts of common law at Westminster, according

to the ancient practice of country attorneys who would not employ an agent to divide their fees."

The reasons given by Lord Campbell for the faith that was in him, besides the legalisms in the plays, are as follows:

" ' Envy does merit as its shade pursue;'

and rivals whom he surpassed, not only envied Shakespeare, but grossly libeled him. Of this we have an example in ' An Epistle to the Gentlemen Students of the Two Universities, by Thomas Nash,' prefixed to the first edition of Robert Greene's 'Menaphon' (which was subsequently called ' Greene's Arcadia '), according to the title page, published in 1589. The alleged libel on Shakespeare is in the words following, viz.:

" ' I will turn back to my first studies of delight, and talk a little in friendship with a few of our trivial translators. It is a common practice nowadays, amongst a sort of shifting companions that run through every art and thrive by none, to leave the trade of *Noverint* whereto they were born, and busy themselves with the endeavors of art, that could scarce Latinize their neck-verse if they should have need; yet English Seneca, read by candle light, yields many good sentences, as *blood is a beggar*, and so forth; and if you entreat him fair in a frosty morning, he will afford you whole *Hamlets;* I should say whole handfuls of tragical speeches. But, O grief! *Tempus edax rerum*—what is it that will last always? The sea exhaled by drops will in continuance be dry; and Seneca, let blood, line by line and page by page, at length must needs die to our stage.'"

The term "Noverint" was applied to lawyers because in Elizabeth's time most legal documents were in Latin, and began "*Noverint universi per presentes.*"

Lord Campbell continues: "In 1592 Greene followed up the attack in his 'Groat's Worth of Wit,' in the following language: 'There is an upstart crow, beautified with our feathers, that with his Tyger's heart wrapped in a player's hide, supposes he is as well able to bombast out a blank verse as the best of you; and being an absolute Johannes Fac-totum, is in his own conceit the only Shakes-scene in a country.'"

Upon these slender threads Lord Campbell hangs these conclusions: "Therefore, my dear Mr. Payne Collier, in support of your opinion that Shakespeare had been bred to the profession of the law in an attorney's office, I think you will be justified in saying that the fact was asserted publicly in Shakespeare's lifetime by two contemporaries of Shakespeare, who were engaged in the same pursuits with himself, who must have known him well, and who were probably acquainted with the whole of his career."

It seems to me impossible for a logical mind to draw such a conclusion. There is no legitimate connection between the two extracts by which it can be asserted that they both refer to the same person. Standing by itself, the quotation from Nash cannot be made to refer to Shakespeare unless the reference to Hamlet has this effect; *while Greene does not refer to him as connected with the Law!*

Nash was notorious for an envious and quarrelsome disposition, and it is idle, and indeed against the known facts, to suppose that Shakespeare was the only dramatist who could excite his animosity. His paper war with Dr. Harvey is one of the bitterest of which we have any record. Referring to this controversy, Sir John Harrington, a contemporary poet, addressed the following verses to Dr. Harvey:

> The proverb says, who fights with dirty foes
> Must needs be foiled, admit they win or lose:
> Then think it does a Doctor's credit dash
> To make himself antagonist to Nash.

Thomas Freeman's *Epigrams*, 1614, contains the following:

OF THOMAS NASH.

> Nash, had Lycambes on earth living been
>   The time thou wast, his death had been all one;
> Had he but moved thy tartest Muse to spleen
>   Unto the fork he had as surely gone:
> For why? there lived not that man, I think,
>   Us'd better or more bitter gall in ink.

A MS. Epitaph runs thus:

> Here lies Tom Nash, that notable railer,
> That in his life ne'er paid Shoemaker or tailor.

In Dekker's " A Knight's Conjuring, Done in Earnest, Discovered in Jest," alluded to above, the

associate poets represented as consorting in the
Elysian fields are Peele, Greene, and Marlowe.

To this company—when it is proposed to enlarge
it by the addition of Nash, that poet is brought in
thus. ". . Whil'st Marlowe, Greene, and Peele
had gotten under the shades of a large vyne, laugh-
ing to see Nash (that was but newly come to their
colledge) still haunted with the sharpe and satyri-
call spirit that followed him here upon earth; for
Nash inveyed bitterly, as he was wont to do," etc.
Such evidences of Nash's bad temper, and the general dislike in which he was held, might be multi-
plied. (See Dodsley's "Old Plays," vol. ix. p. 7.)

Now it is certain that Shakespeare was not "*born*
to the trade of Noverint*"; but the number of contemporary dramatists who are known to have been
connected with the legal profession by birth or education is large as above shown, and any of them
might have excited Nash's envy. Indeed, his hand
seems to have been against every man, and every
man's hand against him.

Nor is the reference to "whole Hamlets" proof
of a reference to Shakespeare. The story of Hamlet appears to have greatly interested the Elizabethan age. Why, it is not so clear. Belleforest's
"translation" of Saxo Grammaticus' "Amleth"
was practically a new work. It was, as anybody
can see from comparing the two versions, about
six times as long.* And it added and padded and
involved the original story to an extraordinary
state of confusion. It was this Belleforest produc-

* See The Bankside Edition of Hamlet—Appendix A.

tion (called Hamlet and not Amleth, because as
Dr. Morgan has pointed out,* Frenchmen as well
as Englishmen transposed their h's), written and
published about 1570, and translated into English,
which, if any, Shakespeare saw. Capell (in the
Introduction to the first volume of his edition of
Shakespeare, p. 52) says, "There can be no doubt
made by persons who are acquainted with these
things, that the translation is not much younger
than the French original."

Shakespeare's son Hamnet (in the Stratford documents published by Halliwell-Phillipps, spelt Am-
blet, Hamlet, and Hamnet) is by many supposed to
have been named for Hamlet; he was born in 1585,
certainly some years before the father could have
written a play on the subject.

Malone (*Variorum*, 1821, vol. ii. p. 372), after
quoting the passage from Nash above referred to,
continues: "Not having seen the first edition of this
tract till a few years ago I formerly doubted
whether the foregoing passage referred to the tragedy of *Hamlet;* but the word *Hamlets* being printed
in the original copy in a different character from the
rest, I have no longer any doubt on the subject.
It is manifest from this passage that some play on
the story of *Hamlet* had been exhibited before the
year 1589; but I am inclined to think that it was
not Shakespeare's drama, but an elder performance,
on which with the aid of the old prose *Historie of
Hamblet*, his tragedy was formed. The great num-

* See " A Study in the Warwickshire Dialect," by Appleton Morgan, etc. (the third edition), p. 41.

ber of pieces which we *know* he formed on the performance of preceding writers, renders it highly
probable that some others also of his dramas were
constructed on plays that are now lost. . . Nash
seems to point at some dramatic writer of that time
who had originally been a scrivener or attorney,
and instead of transcribing deeds and pleadings,
had chosen to imitate Seneca's plays, of which a
translation had been published many years before.
Shakespeare, however freely he may have borrowed
from Plutarch or Holinshed, does not appear to be
at all indebted to Seneca; and I therefore do not
believe he was the person in Nash's contemplation."

Finally, Shakespeare himself said that " Venus
and Adonis," which appeared in 1593, was the
" first heir of [his] invention," and it would seem
therefore that strong proof ought to be required
before assigning an earlier date to any of his plays.

Knight, referring to the same passage in Nash,
says: " Does this description apply to him [Shakes-
peare]? Was he thriving by no art? In 1589 he
was established in life as a sharer in the Black-
friars' theater. Does the term ' whole Hamlets ' fix
the allusion on him? It appears to us only to show
that some tragedy called ' Hamlet,' it may be
Shakespeare's, was then in existence; and that it
was a play also at which Nash might sneer as
abounding in tragical speeches. But it does not
seem that there is any absolute connection between
the noverint and the ' Hamlet.' Suppose, for example, that the ' Hamlet ' alluded to, was written by
Marlowe, who was educated at Cambridge, and

was certainly not a lawyer's clerk. The sentence will read as well; the sarcasm upon the tragical speeches of the 'Hamlet' will be as pointed; the shifting companion who has thriven by no art, and has left the calling to which he was born, may study English Seneca till he produces 'whole Hamlets, I should say handfuls, of tragical speeches.' In the same way Nash might have said whole Tamburlaines of tragical speeches, without attempting to infer that the author of 'Tamburlaine' had left the trade of Noverint. We believe that the allusion was to Shakespeare's 'Hamlet,' but that the first part of the sentence had no allusion to Shakespeare's occupation. The context of the passage renders the matter even clearer. Nash begins, 'I will turn back to my first text of studies of delight, and talk a little in friendship with a few of our trivial translators.' Nash aspired to the reputation of a scholar; and he directs his satire against those who attempted the labors of scholarship without the requisite qualifications. The trivial translators could scarcely latinize their neck-verse—they could scarcely repeat a verse of Scripture, which was the ancient form of praying the benefit of clergy. Seneca, however, might be read in English. We have then to ask, Was 'Hamlet' a translation or an adaptation from Seneca? Did Shakespeare ever attempt to found a play upon the model of Seneca; to be a trivial translator of him; to transfuse his sentences into dramatic composition? If this imputation does not hold good against Shakespeare, the mention of 'Hamlet' has no connection with the shifting companion who is thus talked of as a trivial translator. Nash does not impute these qualities to ' Hamlet,' but to those who busy themselves with the endeavors of art in adapting sentences from Seneca which should rival whole ' Hamlets ' in tragical speeches. 'And then he immediately says, ' But, O grief! *Tempus edax rerum;*—what is it that will last always? The sea exhaled by drops will in continuance be dry; and Seneca, let blood line by line and page by page, at length must needs die to our stage.' "

Lord Campbell himself seems to realize that his readers will not agree with him in his belief that the extract from Nash has any tendency to prove that Shakespeare was ever connected with the law, for, at the end of his book (p. 138), he protests, " I am quite serious in what I have written about Nash and Robert Greene having asserted the fact; but I by no means think that on this ground alone it must necessarily be taken for truth. Their statement that he belonged to the profession of the law may be as false as that he was a plagiarist from Seneca."

Lord Campbell, after giving the quotations above referred to, proceeds to analyze the plays, and finds legal expressions in all but fourteen of the thirty-seven plays usually attributed to Shakespeare.

From the appearance of Lord Campbell's book down to the present time, the work of collecting these legalisms and writing ingenious essays to prove that they exhibit a profound knowledge of the law, has gone on with unremitting zeal, until the conclusion has been reached that Shakespeare was not a mere clerk, but was himself a profound law-yer; and the laborious and learned German Shakes-pearian, Karl Elze, thinks his hero must certainly have been a practicing attorney, because he has found two suits instituted for the recovery of small sums of money, wherein Shakespeare was the plaintiff, and in which no attorney's appearance is entered, and that accordingly, Shakespeare must have conducted them himself; while other scholars have gone so far as to assert that no less a lawyer than Francis Bacon could have written the plays.

III.

SOME LATER CONVERTS TO THE SHAKESPEARE-LAWYER DOCTRINE.

By far the ablest and most comprehensive contribution to the subject of Shakespeare's legal acquirements has been made by that eminent lawyer and statesman, Senator Cushman K. Davis, whose work of over three hundred pages was published in 1884, quickly went through two editions and is now out of print. Senator Davis attaches no importance to Nash's reference to " Noverint "; but bases his argument entirely upon the internal evidence of the plays and poems. In all he finds that law terms have been used 312 times; but as he enumerates each repeated use of the same word, and as nearly all of them are used more than once, and many as often as four or five times, the number of distinct legal expressions is very much less. And there is a strained effort to discover legalisms where the average reader, even though he be a lawyer, would least suspect them; and to swell the list many words cited are not strictly legal words at all, *e. g.*,

> Having ever seen in the prenominate crimes,
> The youth you breathe of, guilty, be assured.
>   —" Hamlet," Act II. scene 1.

Senator Davis' comment is: " Prenominate " is the synonym of " aforesaid."

> . . . See thou render this
> Unto my cousin's hand, Doctor Bellario.
> —" Merchant of Venice," Act III. scene 4.

Here " render " is forced into service because " rendering and yielding as rent " is the phrase in leases.

Among other words given as illustrations of legalisms are: bourn, edict, traitor, pardon, reprieve, respite, writ, oath, bail, execution, outlawry, verdict, jointure, dowry, attainder, distrained, inheritance, warrant (" There's law and warrant, lady, for my curse," " King John," Act II. scene 1), tenement, last will and testament, etc. The frequent use of such words can have no tendency to prove a knowledge of law.

On the other hand, Senator Davis points out numerous instances where legal terms are correctly used with their strictly technical meanings; and he bases a strong argument on the cumulative effect of such repeated instances. Just how many of these there are it is a matter of some difficulty to say, as they are scattered through the book in the midst of such words as are mentioned above, which are not used in any legal or technical sense; but I believe they do not number over twenty-five or thirty.

He further argues that " Shakespeare has a lawyer's conservatism. He respected the established order of things. . . There is nowhere [in his works] a hint of sympathy with personal rights as against the sovereign, nor with parliament, then first assuming its protective attitude toward the English people. . . In all his works there is not one direct word for liberty of speech, thought, religion—those rights which in his age were the very seeds of time, into which his eye of all men's could best look to see which would grow and which would not."

To say that this spirit of "uncompromising feudalism" indicates a legal training is to make an assertion in the very teeth of history. Coke's spirit, which resisted the prerogative, which upheld the common law and chartered rights of the people, which maintained the equality of all men in the eye of the law, was and is typical of the lawyer. This is the "conservatism" which education in the law breeds in its devotees. All history proves it. That Shakespeare had none of this conservatism, that in "'King John' he ignored the Magna Charta, that he ever and always shows a patrician contempt for popular rights"—this proves, if it proves anything, that he had not a legal training.

I believe an equal labor, an equally microscopic examination of the dramas, an equally ingenious application of all the references to medicine would prove with as much certainty that their author was a physician; but, so far as I am aware, none of the numerous writers upon his medical knowledge has as yet asserted that he either practiced or studied the science of Galen, to whom he so often refers.

That his use of military expressions proves Shakespeare to have been a soldier has been seriously contended. (See W. J. Thoms's "Notelets on Shakespeare," London, 1865.)

IV.

AN ENGLISH QUEEN'S COUNSEL'S REMARKABLE OPINION.

BUT most wonderful pronouncement of all, Mr. Edward James Castle, Q. C., in 1897 prints a book —" Shakespeare, Bacon, Jonson, and Greene "—in which he completely falls under the *umbra* of Lord Campbell as to the value and significance of these " legalisms " in the Plays. Mr. Castle divides Shakespeare's dramas into *legal* and *non-legal* plays, discovering, or professing to discover, vast legal lore in the former and ignorance of the law in the latter. In his Introduction he states that his studies upon the subject were not made with a view to support a theory. But it would appear that, when Mr. Castle came to write his book, his " discovery " (to use his own word) warped his judgment.

For even assuming that his theory is correct, that some plays show knowledge and others ignorance of law; Mr. Castle's conclusion that the former *must* have been or even probably were the joint production of Shakespeare and Bacon, or some other lawyer, who worked together as Beaumont and Fletcher did, is certainly a *non sequitur*. Writers of all times, when treating of technical subjects, have been wont to consult and take the advice of men skilled in those subjects; the novelist who introduces medical or legal subjects consults with a physician or lawyer—sometimes he correctly uses the knowledge he thus acquires, and sometimes he does not. Or, without consulting a specialist, he may have some familiarity with technical terms, and may use them with accuracy or otherwise.

Mr. Castle's efforts to show real legal knowledge in the plays are labored in the extreme. The first instance he gives of legalisms fairly illustrates them all, and my criticism upon it is fairly applicable to them all. Shakespeare uses the word "color" as · meaning "apparent, not real," which is its significa- tion when used as a law term. Mr. Castle devotes five pages of his work to detailing the various technical refinements drawn by the old lawyers in regard to "giving color" in pleadings, and assumes that, because "color" is used with its legal mean- ing, it must have been a lawyer who so used it, and that he knew all these technical refinements—an unwarranted presumption even in the case of a pro- fessional lawyer. Color, in its application to plead- ing, was, I believe, abolished in England by the pro- cedure act of 1852, and this may be some excuse for Mr. Castle's admitted ignorance (p. 20) on the sub- ject, but it is still in force in all states where the common-law procedure is in vogue, and the average lawyer, who knows little or nothing of the refine- ments in its use mentioned by Mr. Castle, refers to it familiarly in his everyday practice. But the use of the word color was not confined to the science of pleading; it was and still is used in other applications with practically the same meaning: as " color of title," a title *prima facie* good, but for some reason, not apparent on its face, not good in fact; and " color of office," as where an act is done by an officer under pretense that it is within his authority, when in truth it is not, it is said to be done under color of office, *colore officii*. The use of the word color in its legal sense of " apparent, not real " cannot certainly indicate profound knowledge of law, and it *is simply absurd* to assume that the mere use of a technical legal term by Shakespeare indicates that he had a knowledge of all the hair-splitting logic which the ancient doctors of the common law used in *applying* legal doctrines and terms to particular cases. The " rule in Shelley's case " any lawyer can define, but of its application in particular cases every lawyer is doubtful; the average layman is familiar with the phrase, but, according to Mr. Castle's logic, if a lay writer uses it this fact indicates that he is a profound lawyer and has a knowledge of all the vast learning and ingenious logic used in the application of the rule and embodied in *many volumes* of reports and text-books.

Shakespeare, in common with his contemporaries and in common with observant men for many centuries previous to his time, knew that all terrestial bodies are attracted toward the center of the earth, and he several times refers to this fact; we must therefore believe, if we follow Mr. Castle's mental processes, that Shakespeare was familiar with the law of gravitation and all its applications; that he knew Newton's and Kepler's laws and all modern astronomy. Old Capulet calls Juliet's fine distinction between being proud of the County Paris and being thankful for him—"chop logic." * I know of no other term so apt and appropriate to apply to Mr. Castle's book.

But if he was unfortunate in his efforts to discover legal knowledge in the " legal " plays, he becomes positively puerile when he undertakes to prove lack of such knowledge in the " non-legal " plays. After a careful search through the many pages devoted to this part of his work I have failed to discover *a single instance* given by him of any real blunder in the use of legal terms. The following quotations fairly illustrate his arguments here:

> " ' Plead my successive title with your swords.'

" It is incongruous to speak of *pleading* with swords. Grotius speaks of the antagonism between the law and arms; how in times of peace the former, and in war the latter, prevail. *Cedant arma togæ* is the maxim for the first; *Inter arma sileant* [sic] *leges* for the second.

" ' Successive title ' even shows more strongly want of legal training. Malone indeed, interprets it as meaning ' my title to the succession '; no doubt this is its meaning, but successive title means one title succeeding another, as successive waves, etc., and might perhaps be used where independent titles

---

* " Romeo and Juliet," III. v. 150. The late Mr. S. S. Cox once referred to the speech of a fellow-congressman as " chopstick logic," which is even more appropriate.

follow one another; a somewhat difficult thing to conceive, as a title is continuous.

> " ' But yet I'll make assurance doubly sure
> And take a bond of fate.'

" It is impossible to see, even by way of metaphor, how killing Macduff is taking a bond of fate. . . It is mere sound, not sense, and the word is wrongly used.

> " ' Our high-placed Macbeth
> Shall live the lease of nature, pay his breath
> To time and mortal custom.'

" What mortal custom means it is difficult to say, unless perhaps, customary or common mortality. But it should be the lease *from* nature."

How utterly inane and childish such criticism is! And yet Mr. Castle gives no better illustrations than these to prove Shakespeare's ignorance of law in what he calls the " non-legal " plays.

The reader will notice that most of the instances hereinafter given of Shakespeare's mistakes in the use of legal terms are taken from Mr. Castle's " legal plays," to wit, " Hamlet," " Richard III.," " Henry VIII.," and " 3 Henry VI.," etc.

V.

SOME OF SHAKESPEARE'S ERRORS IN LEGAL. TERMINOLOGY.

FOR my part I see no profound knowledge of law displayed in the plays. It would indeed be strange, considering the surroundings of Shakespeare's birth and education, if he did not make frequent use of legal expressions. Could the universal genius, who apparently like his own creation, Posthumus Leonatus, had

> " All the learnings, that his time
> Could make him the receiver of: which he took
> As we do air,"

have been brought up as it were within the four walls of a court house, with the litigants, jurors, and lawyers his daily companions, and have failed to absorb, aye, drink in as he did the air, digest and make his own, a large fund of the legal lore of his surroundings? On the contrary, for him not to have done so would be a matter of infinite surprise.

To me it seems that it ought to be apparent to any lawyer, who is not an enthusiast, that Shakespeare's knowledge of law was simply a knowledge of legal expressions, with a fairly correct idea of their application such as any bright man attending court frequently and in daily companionship with lawyers could not fail to acquire; and that of the law itself he had no real knowledge, except such little as he could pick up in the manner indicated.

Though the frequent use of legal terms, with their proper technical meanings, has a cumulative effect, and tends strongly to prove a legal training; yet a very few errors in such use, if glaring and gross, would absolutely nullify that effect and proof. Without presuming to rival the learning and ingenuity, the patience and labor bestowed by Lord Campbell and Senator Davis, I have collected some instances of inaccuracy in the use of law-terms which I believe destroy the force of their reasoning.

> Tell me what state, what dignity, what honor
> Canst thou demise to any child of mine ?
> > —" Richard III.," Act IV. scene 4.

Dignities and honors could not be demised.—3 Comyn's Dig. Tit. Dignity (E), 2 Bl. Com. 36, 37.

> Besides, to be demanded of a sponge ! What replication
> Should be made by the son of a king ?
> > —" Hamlet," Act IV. scene 2.

A very few days, or, at most, weeks, of practical training in a lawyer's office would have sufficed to teach Shakespeare that this is an incorrect use of the word replication. The course of pleading is as follows: The plaintiff makes his demand on the defendant by a narratio or declaration; the defendant replies by a plea; and the *plaintiff's* reply to this plea is called a replication. Certainly comment is here unnecessary. Apparently Shakespeare determined to make use of a legal expression even if he had to do violence to it, to commit an assault on it, as it were, and lug it in by the ears. And the same may be said of some of the other instances hereafter given. Shakespeare's was a learned and a pedantic age, and while he could not rival his more plodding contemporaries in their labored efforts to weigh down their works with classical allusions, none of them at all rivaled him in his knowledge of, and his reference to, that great world around him— all that he could see and hear. He knew the habits of birds and insects, the properties of herbs and flowers, and besides, soon had a grasp of all the knowledge of that brilliant gathering of playwrights, his contemporaries and associates, among whom were lawyers, physicians, divines, and nearly all of whom were classical scholars. Like Leonatus he took his " learnings " as we do air; he breathed it in; he absorbed it; he did not get it out of books. This is what Milton means when he contrasts Jonson's with Shakespeare's learning:

> " Then to the well-trod stage anon,
> If Jonson's learned sock be on,
> Or sweetest Shakespeare, Fancy's child,
> Warble his native woodnotes wild."

But legal expressions are highly technical, and when Shakespeare attended those feasts of the law in courts and in gatherings of attorneys, and carried away scraps, it is not at all surprising that he should occasionally commit an error when he used them so frequently. And when, in a comparatively few instances, his applications of law terms are so highly technical and so correctly given as to sug-

gest a lawyer's touch, can we not readily believe
that here he took advice of some lawyer friend?
In the very nature of things he must have had many
such friends.

Till you compound whose right is worthiest
We, for the worthiest, will hold the right from both.
>—" King John," Act II. scene 1.

And we here deliver,
Subscribed by the consuls and patricians,
Together with the seal o' the senate, what
We have compounded on.
>—" Coriolanus," Act V. scene 6.

Content you, gentlemen; I will compound this strife;
'Tis deeds must win the prize; and, he of both,
That can assure my daughter greatest dower
Shall have Bianca's love.
>—" The Taming of the Shrew," Act II. scene 1.

To compound (though cited as a legalism by
Senator Davis) is in all these cases used in the general sense of to settle or determine; but, in a legal
sense, it is to settle in a particular manner, as where
a creditor agrees to receive part of his debt in satisfaction of the whole; or, in criminal law, where one
receives a consideration to refrain from prosecuting
a wrongdoer, as when one whose goods have been
stolen agrees not to prosecute the thief if the goods
are returned, which is called " compounding a felony," where the theft amounted to a felony. To-
day, in general literature, the word is used in pretty
much the same sense in which Shakespeare uses it
—perhaps this is due to the force of his great
example.

For if a king'bid a man be a villain, he is bound by the indenture of his oath to be one.

—"Pericles," Act I. scene 3.

Here the oath of allegiance is referred to. The use of the word "indenture" is entirely out of place.

" 'An indenture' was a writing containing a conveyance, bargain, or contract . . . between two or more parties, consisting of the same matter written twice or oftener on the same sheet with a space between, where, after execution, the parchment was cut in a serrated or indented line, and a part delivered to each of the parties."—*Burrill's Law Dictionary.*

The word indenture has survived to modern times, though actual indenting or cutting is never done; but in Shakespeare's time it seems actual indenting was necessary to constitute an "indenture" (5 Co., 21, Stile's Case), and it was so in Maryland until 1794, when it was abolished by chapter 57 of the Acts of that year.

An oath never (and *ex vi termini* not an oath of allegiance, it being unilateral) had anything to do do with an indenture or an indenture with an oath.

Glend. Come, here's the map; shall we divide our right
According to our threefold order ta'en ?

Mort. The archdeacon hath divided it
Into three limits very equally.

. . . . .

Hot. Me thinks my moiety, north from Burton here,
In quantity equals not one of yours.

—"I Henry IV.," Act III. scene I.

Moiety (L. Lat. *mediatas*) does not mean a third. A half; one of two equal parts.—Co. Litt. 34 a, b.

It is to be noted, however, that some modern law-yers and text-writers use the word moiety as inac-curately as Shakespeare, as though it could mean a third, or any part.

> I do believe,
> Induced by potent circumstances, that
> You are my enemy, and make my challenge.
> You shall not be my judge;
>
> . . . . .
>
> I do refuse you for my judge, and here
> Before you all, appeal unto the pope.
> —" Henry VIII.," Act II. scene 4.

To " challenge " is to object or except to those who are returned to act as *jurors*, either individ-ually or collectively as a body. The *judge* was not subject to challenge.

> In which our valiant Hamlet—
> For so this side of our known world esteemed him—
> Did slay this Fortinbras ; who by a sealed compact,
> Well ratified by law and heraldry,
> Did forfeit with his life. . .
> —" Hamlet," Act I. scene 1.

Here " well ratified by " means " strictly in ac-cordance with." As a legalism its use is out of place.

" Ratification is where a person adopts a con-tract or other transaction which is not binding on him because entered into by an unauthorized agent. Thus, if A enters into a contract on behalf of B, without having B's authority to do so, B may either repudiate or adopt the contract; if he adopts it he is said to ratify it, and it then takes effect as if it had been originally made by his authority."— *Rapalje & Lawrence's Law Dic.*

Therefore our sometime sister, now our queen,
The imperial jointress to this warlike State. . .
—" Hamlet," Act I. scene 2.

" Jointress, a woman who has an estate settled on her by her husband, to hold during her life if she survive him."—*Co. Litt. 46.*

Jointure was one of the means used for barring dower. It was an estate settled on the wife before marriage, and in lieu of dower; if made after marriage, upon the husband's death the widow could either accept it or reject it and take her dower at common law (2 Bl. Comm. 137).

Queen Gertrude could have neither a dower nor a jointure in the kingdom of Denmark.

Boyet. So you grant pasture for me [*offering to kiss her.*]
Mar. Not so, gentle beast;
My lips no common are, though several they be.
—" Love's Labor Lost," Act II. scene 1.

Shakespeare doubtless knew that one cannot at the same time hold a thing in common and in severalty, and if so, he here sacrifices his knowledge for a mere play on words, which I fancy a professional pride, if he had had any legal training, would not have permitted him to do.

· *War.* Why should you sigh, my lord?
King H. Not for myself, Lord Warwick, but my son,
Whom I unnaturally shall disinherit.

But be it as it may: I here entail
The crown to thee, and to thine heirs forever;
Conditionally that thou here take an oath
To cease this civil war, and, whilst I live,
To honor me as thy king and sovereign;
And neither by treason, nor hostility,
To seek to put me down and reign thyself.
                    —" 3 Henry VI.," Act I. scene 1.

Senator Davis admits an inaccuracy here. I
quote his language (p. 199): " This is an attempt to
grant the crown, subject to a condition subsequent.
The use of the word entail here seems to be inac-
curate, for, though the use of the word heirs is
necessary to create a fee, so the word ' body ' or
some other words of procreation are necessary to
make it a fee tail. A gift to a man and his heirs,
male or female, is an estate in fee simple and not
in fee tail " (2 Bl. Comm., 114).

You three, Biron, Dumain, and Longaville,
Have sworn for three years' term to live with me,
My fellow scholars, and to keep those statutes
That are recorded in this schedule here.
Your oaths are passed, and now subscribe your names.
                    —" Love's Labor's Lost," Act I. scene 1.

The word " statutes " is here used to mean simply
articles of agreement. It has no such meaning in
law. A statute is an act of the legislature of a
country. "Statutes-merchant" and "statutes-
staple " were the names of certain securities for debt
in Shakespeare's time, and perhaps this gave him
the idea that any agreement might be called a
statute.

Adr. Why, man, what is the matter?
Dro. S. I do not know the matter: he is 'rested on the case.
— " The Comedy of Errors," Act IV. scene 2.

He was not arrested " on the case." Civil actions at law are broadly divided into two classes: actions *ex contractu,* growing out of breach of contract, either express or implied, and actions *ex delicto,* for the recovery for wrongs independent of contract. The suit against Antipholus was of the former class, being for the recovery of the price of goods purchased from the jeweler; an action on the case is one of the actions *ex delicto.*

Antipholus was actually placed under arrest upon the simple statement of the jeweler to an officer that the former was indebted to him, without writ, warrant, or any process whatever.

Sec. Mer. Therefore make present satisfaction, or I'll Attach you by this officer.

.   .   .   .   .

Well, officer, arrest him at my suit,

Ang. Either consent to pay the sum for me,
Or I attach you by this officer.
Here is thy fee ; arrest him, officer.
— " The Comedy of Errors," Act IV. scene 1.

Justice must be administered in a very primitive style, where one who claims that another is indebted to him can call an officer and say, " Here, officer, this man owes me money; arrest him." Lawyers and courts would be unnecessary, and no one could complain of the law's delay where such a summary method of procedure was permitted.

> *Cant.*   For all the temporal lands, which men devout
> By testament have given to the church,
> Would they strip from us.
> —" Henry V.," Act I. scene 1.

The use of the word " testament " is here incorrect. A testator bequeaths *personal* property by a " testament "; he devises real estate by a " will."

> *Antony.*   Moreover he hath left you all his walks,
> His private arbors, and his new planted orchards,
> On this side Tiber, he hath left them you,
> And to your heirs forever.
> —" Julius Cæsar," Act III. scene 2.

In regard to this passage Senator Davis says: " It is to be remarked that Antony, in speaking of the real estate left by Cæsar to the Roman people, does not use the appropriate word ' devise.' Shakespeare nowhere uses the word in connection with a will. It was also unnecessary for Cæsar's will to have contained the expression ' to your heirs forever ' in order to give the people a perpetual estate in the reality."

> *Shylock.*   Go with me to a notary ; seal me there
> Your single bond, and in a merry sport
> If you repay me not on such a day,
> In such a place, such sum or sums as are
> Expressed in the condition, let the forfeit
> Be nominated for an equal pound
> Of your fair flesh, to be cut off and taken
> In what part of your body it pleaseth me.
> —" Merchant of Venice," Act I. scene 3.

It is hardly conceivable that any lawyer, or anyone who had spent a considerable time in a lawyer's office, in Shakespeare's age, could have been guilty of the egregious error of calling a bond with a collateral condition a " single bond." A single bond, *simplex obligatio,* is a bond without a collateral condition, but that described by Shylock is with collateral condition. It is possible that a lawyer in this age would be guilty of ignorance on this point; but hardly in Elizabeth's age, and least of all a lawyer in an inland town like Stratford. In our time, the use of sealed instruments except in cases of contracts in reference to real estate, contracts by corporations, and bonds with collateral condition, has largely ceased among merchants and business men generally, though still in frequent use by lawyers. This disuse of sealed instruments is, perhaps, chiefly due to the extension of the *lex mercatoria,* and the advantage of negotiability that pertains to most unsealed instruments, and is also undoubtedly largely due to the fact that almost all men can write their names, and that not to be able to do so is considered a disgrace. Certain legal incidents, for historical reasons, still attach to sealed instruments; but, for practical business purposes, the private seal is now a useless survival of the Middle Ages. Its use has been abolished by statute in most of the Western States. But in Shakespeare's time the situation was entirely different. The seal was in universal use. Indeed it is beyond dispute that sometimes educated men belonging to the gentry, instead of writing their names themselves, would prefer to have them written by the draughtsman of the instrument which they were to sign and would themselves simply affix their seals, as being distinctive of their house or family; and tradesmen who could write would merely make their marks, they being generally distinctive of their trade or calling. The probability is that in the small town of Stratford, having little or no commerce with the outside world, the use of the promissory note, bill of exchange, or any unsealed instrument was entirely unknown to its business people. Accordingly, it must be assumed that the difference between a single bond and a bond with a collateral condition was thoroughly understood by every lawyer and every lawyer's clerk in Stratford.

But in this play, Shakespeare not only manifests his lack of knowledge of the technique of the legal profession; he shows a profound ignorance of law and of the fundamental principles of justice—unless we assume that the trial scene disregards all ideas of law, justice, and morality for mere dramatic effect; but it has been repeatedly shown by many writers that equal dramatic effect could have been attained without such sacrifice.

Portia, as *amicus curiæ*, or referee, in "The Merchant of Venice" makes five distinct rulings which are bad in law, in logic, and in morals.* Shy-

---

* See "Shakespeare in Fact and in Criticism," Appleton Morgan ; New York, Benjamin, 1888, p. 180. To make these errors more apparent, Dr. Morgan imagines the case of Shylock and Antonio, as decided by Portia, sent back for a new trial before Portia, and finally as reversed, as to every one of her rulings, by a full bench on appeal.

lock sues for the penalty under his bond. Portia
decides that the contract is lawful, and that he has a
right to the penalty. *Ex turpe causa non oritur
actio* was a maxim of the Civil as well as the Common law. Shakespeare was himself apparently
familiar with it, for in " Henry VI.," Part II. Act
V. Scene 1, he says:

> " Who canst be bound by any solemn vow
> To do a murderous deed, to rob a man," etc.

The action could no more have been sustained in
Venice than it could in England. Yet Portia
awards judgment.

> " A pound of that same merchant's flesh is thine,
> The court awards it, and the law doth give it."

But she adds:

> " Tarry a little, there is something else.
> The bond doth give thee here no jot of blood,
> The words expressly are, a pound of flesh;
> Then take thy bond, take thou thy pound of flesh,
> But, in the cutting it, if thou dost shed
> One drop of Christian blood, thy lands and goods
> Are by the laws of Venice confiscate
> Unto the State."

Well might Shylock exclaim " Is that the law? "
Whoever heard of flesh without blood? A fig
without seeds, a nut without a shell?

The court, having pronounced judgment and
awarded execution, tells Shylock that he must
himself execute the judgment. He might well have
answered, " I have come here for the court to give
me justice, not to take the law in my own hands.

I am not an officer of the court; let the court's officers execute its judgment, and let them be responsible for failure to do so properly. Even if the
court gave a judgment for so much money I should
perhaps render myself liable in an action for dam-
ages if I attempted to collect it myself. It would
be the business of the court, through its own officers, to collect my money, and it is the business
and duty of the court to deliver me my pound of
flesh. I have no right to take it myself, and no
court of justice can have the legal power or moral
right to make a suitor therein responsible for the
execution of its judgments."

But the next ruling is more remarkable than the
former. Shylock says he will accept the tender of
thrice the bond; but Portia answers " Thou shall
have nothing but the penalty," and

> " If thou tak'st more
> Or less than a just pound, be it so much
> As makes it light or heavy in the substance
> Or the division of the twentieth part
> Of one poor scruple, nay, if the scale do turn
> But in the estimation of a hair,
> Thou diest, and all thy goods are confiscate."

Can one imagine it being a criminal act for a
creditor to take less than the amount due him?

And, to cap the climax, this remarkable judge
then rules that Shylock has forfeited the principal
of his debt because he refused a tender. The
climax? No; that was still to come. The court
quickly resolves itself into one of criminal jurisdiction, and the Jew's goods and life are declared for-

feit: and for what? For having dared to make a contract which that same court had a moment before declared valid and binding. And finally this judge, who had given utterance to that eloquent appeal for mercy, stands by while the Jew is required, on pain of forfeiture of his life, to abandon the cherished religion of his fathers and his race, and embrace the hated religion of the Christian— an ingenuity of cruelty surpassing that of the thumbscrew or the rack. And all this; the three thousand ducats he had lent, all his property, and all the property which he might afterward acquire (for he was required to record in court a deed of gift of all he died possessed), his religion, and even his life—all forfeited because he had made a contract which the court held was valid and could be enforced.

And, by the way, this deed of gift is another blunder in law. It is a fixed principle of the common law that a man cannot convey a thing which he has not, though he afterward acquire it. Only things *in esse*, having an actual or potential existence, were subjects capable of gift or grant (Comyn's Dig. Tit: *Grant* (D)).

It has been suggested to the author of these papers that this deed of gift might have been valid as a gift *causa mortis*, or as a Will. But of course no lawyer need be told that it has not a single element necessary to the validity of a gift *causa mortis*, either under the Civil or Common law. Cooper's Justinian (ed. 1852), pp. 100, 476.

To be sure instruments in the form of deeds have

frequently been construed to be wills under the Common Law. "There is nothing that requires so little solemnity," said Lord Hardwick (in Ross *vs.* Ewen, 3 Atkins, 163), "as making a Will of personal property, for there is scarcely any writing which will not be admitted as such." In Maryland in 1883 a letter written by a decedent to his daughter was held to be a valid will of personalty (Byers *vs.* Hoppe, 61 Md. 206). Indeed, any writing signed by the party making a disposition of property to take effect after death, whether in the form of a deed, or whatever its form, might or could be construed to be a will. It would appear, however, that this was not so by the Civil law. By it certain particular formalities were necessary in the making of a will (Cooper's Justinian, Ed. 1852, p. 112, *et seq.*), and it is therefore improbable that a paper executed as a deed of gift, could, under that system, be adjudged to be a will. But Shylock's deed of gift of "all he died possessed" would not have been valid as a will of real estate which he might acquire after the date of its execution, any more than it would have been as a deed of gift as to "after-acquired" property. Other reasons of a technical nature might be given why this deed could not have taken effect as a will either under the Common law or the Civil law of Venice. But they are unnecessary. The deed of gift which Shylock was required to execute was not his voluntary act, and it is a contradiction in terms to speak of an involuntary act as a will or testament (which latter word is essentially identical in meaning with

" will "). *Testamentum ex eo appellatur, quod testatio mentis sit.*

This deed of gift was required to be recorded " here in the court." The recital of such an instrument (for a paper in the form of a deed always shows the consideration or cause of its execution) would show on its face that it was executed in pursuance of a decree of the court, and not by the voluntary act of the party.

The court which passed upon Shylock's case did not observe the distinction of England between courts of law and equity, but assumed to act as both (indeed, it also assumed criminal jurisdiction). Now, a court of equity originally acted wholly by decrees *in personam*, and enforced its decrees in no other way than by fine and imprisonment for disobedience. Where, therefore, one obeys such a decree, he cannot be said to act voluntarily.

Waiving, however, all fine distinctions, I conclude: If Shakespeare desired to show his knowledge of law by indicating that a paper in the form of a deed may be considered a will; the method he uses to do so, of itself, shows gross ignorance of the fundamental principles of the law. Assuming that this was Shakespeare's intention, he—in effect —makes the court order and decree Shylock to execute a will, and file it in the court. If any court ever had such power, this is, I believe, the only recorded instance of its exercise. But it is an absurdity in terms. Assuming, however, that the court had the power, its exercise would be futile, for, if the deed which Shylock executed was in fact

a will, he could immediately afterwards have re-
voked it and made a new and last Will and Testament, thereby defeating the object of Portia's decree—a thing which could not be within the pur-
view of the dramatic action of the Play. Portia's
object was to compel Shylock to execute a paper
which would have the finality of a judicial action.
It is the last will that counts, just as in the case of
deeds, it is the first.

Of course, if Shylock died intestate, Jessica
would inherit or succeed to his property, provided
he did not afterwards remarry, and have other children; in which case she would only have taken her
pro rata share. But what would happen in case of
intestacy is not under discussion. The question is,
was the paper valid either as a will or as a deed?
The result is that Portia's effort to vest Jessica
(who had married a Christian) with Shylock's
estate, real and personal, was as abortive and as
ridiculous as any or all of her judicial pronounce-
ments. Lawyers who, like my Lord Campbell and
Senator Davis, desire to swear Shakespeare in as a
lawyer learned in the law had best omit consideration of " The Merchant of Venice."

I cannot close my reference to the law of this
play better than by quoting again from Von Ihering:

" The truth remains truth, even when the indi-
vidual defends it only from the narrow point of view
of his personal interests. It is hatred and revenge
that takes Shylock before the Court to cut his
pound of flesh out of Antonio's body; but the words

which the poet puts into his mouth are as true in it
as in any other. It is the language which the
wounded feeling of legal right will speak, in all
times and in all places; the power, the firmness of
the conviction, that law must remain Law, the lofty
feeling and pathos of a man who is conscious that,
in what he claims, there is a question not only of
his person but of The Law. ' The pound of flesh,'
Shakespeare makes him say:

> " ' The pound of flesh which I demand of him,
> Is dearly bought, is mine, and I will have it;
> If you deny me, fie upon your law;
> There is no force in the decrees of Venice.
>   . . . I crave the law.
>   . . . I stay here upon my bond.'

" ' I crave the law.' In these four words, the
poet has described the relation of the law, in the
subjective, to law in the objective sense of the term:
and the meaning of ' The Struggle for Law,' in a
manner better than any philosopher of the law
could have done it. These four words change Shylock's claim into a question of the Law of Venice.
To what mighty, giant dimensions does not the
weak man grow, when he speaks these words! It
is no longer the Jew demanding his pound of flesh;
it is the Law of Venice itself, knocking at the door
of justice; for his Rights and the Law of Venice
are one and the same; they must stand or fall
together."

We feel little pity for Shylock, but our sense of
reverence for the law is shocked—the majesty of
the Law is degraded.

Thus I believe I have shown, though in a very brief and imperfect way, that Shakespeare had no knowledge of the technique of law, and no just appreciation of those fundamental principles of justice which are the basis of all law. Though he excelled all other men who have ever lived in knowledge of, and in ability to portray, human nature in all its aspects, his ideas of human rights were narrow and bigoted.

It has been said that Englishmen for generations took their religion from Milton, and their history from Shakespeare; but for their law they have looked and must look to an entirely different class of men.

THE END.